HOW TO REDUCE ENVIRONMENTAL POLLUTION BY CREATING A NEW MATERIAL TO REPLACE PLASTIC

How to Reduce Environmental Pollution by Creating a New Material to Replace Plastic

Walter the Educator

Silent King Books
A WhichHead Entertainment Imprint

Copyright © 2024 by Walter the Educator

All rights reserved. No part of this book may be reproduced in any manner whatsoever without written permission except in the case of brief quotations embodied in critical articles and reviews.

First Printing, 2024

Disclaimer

The author and publisher offer this information without warranties expressed or implied. No matter the grounds, neither the author nor the publisher will be accountable for any losses, injuries, or other damages caused by the reader's use of this book. Your use of this book acknowledges an understanding and acceptance of this disclaimer.

How to Reduce Environmental Pollution by Creating a New Material to Replace Plastic is a little problem solver book by Walter the Educator that belongs to the Little Problem Solver Books Series.
Collect them all and more books at WaltertheEducator.com

LITTLE PROBLEM
SOLVER BOOKS

INTRO

The prevalence of plastic in everyday life is undeniable. From packaging and containers to automotive parts and electronics, plastic has become an essential part of the modern economy. However, the durability and convenience of plastic come with a significant environmental cost. Each year, millions of tons of plastic waste are discarded into the environment, where they accumulate in landfills and oceans, wreaking havoc on ecosystems and wildlife. Moreover, plastics are typically derived from non-renewable fossil fuels, contributing to carbon emissions during their production and disposal.

With rising awareness of environmental pollution and the urgent need to mitigate its impact, developing alternatives to plastic has become a priority for scientists, engineers, and innovators. Creating new materials that can replace plastic while offering comparable functionality, durability, and cost-effectiveness could be the key to reducing environmental pollution. This little book explores the concept of creating a new material to replace plastic and outlines the scientific, technical, and environmental considerations required to reduce pollution effectively.

1. The Urgent Need to Replace Plastic

To understand why replacing plastic is critical, it is essential to examine the environmental consequences of plastic pollution:

- **Long degradation period**: Plastic takes centuries to decompose. Some types, such as polyethylene (used in plastic bags), can persist for 500 to 1,000 years in landfills. As a result, every piece of plastic ever created still exists in some form, accumulating and causing long-term environmental damage.

- **Harm to marine life**: Millions of tons of plastic end up in the oceans every year, where they break down into microplastics. These tiny particles are ingested by marine animals, leading to malnutrition, reproductive issues, and death. Ultimately, microplastics enter the human food chain, posing unknown health risks.

- **Greenhouse gas emissions**: The production of plastic is energy-intensive and relies heavily on petrochemicals, contributing to global carbon emissions. Additionally, when plastics are incinerated, they release harmful gases, further exacerbating air pollution.

Given the vast scale of plastic production and the difficulties of managing plastic waste, the need for an environmentally friendly alternative is clear. The solution lies in developing new materials that can perform the functions of plastic while reducing pollution, waste accumulation, and environmental degradation.

2. Principles of Creating a New Material to Replace Plastic

Developing a new material to replace plastic requires an interdisciplinary approach that draws upon materials science, chemistry, biology, and engineering. To be a viable alternative, this material must meet several key criteria:

1. **Sustainability**: The new material should be derived from renewable or abundant natural resources to minimize dependence on non-renewable fossil fuels. It should also be biodegradable or recyclable to prevent accumulation in the environment.
2. **Durability**: While the new material should degrade under environmental conditions, it must also be strong and durable enough for everyday use. This ensures it can replace plastic in various applications without compromising performance.
3. **Non-toxic**: The new material should not release harmful chemicals during its production, use, or disposal. Many plastics contain additives that can leach into food or water, posing health risks. An ideal replacement would avoid these issues altogether.
4. **Cost-effectiveness**: To be adopted on a large scale, the new material must be affordable to produce and process. Plastics are widely used because of their low cost, so any alternative must be competitively priced.
5. **Versatility**: Plastic's success lies in its versatility, being used in applications ranging from packaging and textiles to medical devices and electronics. A new material must be adaptable and capable of fulfilling the broad range of plastic's current roles.

With these principles in mind, the process of inventing a new material can be broken down into several stages, from selecting appropriate raw materials to testing performance and environmental impact.

3. Selecting Sustainable Raw Materials

The first step in creating a new material is identifying the right raw materials. Many existing bioplastics and biodegradable materials are derived from renewable sources such as plants, algae, and fungi. The challenge is to find materials that are abundant, easy to grow, and can be processed efficiently.

- **Plant-based polymers**: Many bioplastics are made from plant-based polymers such as starch, cellulose, and polylactic acid (PLA). These polymers are derived from crops like corn, sugarcane, and potatoes, making them renewable and biodegradable. For example, PLA is already used in products such as food packaging, disposable cutlery, and 3D printing.
- **Algae-based materials**: Algae offer several advantages as a raw material for plastic alternatives. Algae grow rapidly, require minimal resources, and can be cultivated in various environments, including freshwater, saltwater, and wastewater. Additionally, algae can absorb carbon dioxide during growth, contributing to a reduction in greenhouse gas emissions. Researchers are exploring the potential of algae-based polymers for creating biodegradable films, packaging, and other products.
- **Fungal materials**: Fungi, particularly mycelium (the root structure of mushrooms), have garnered attention as a sustainable alternative to plastic. Mycelium can grow into complex, durable structures and can be molded into various shapes. It is fully biodegradable and can be used to create packaging, insulation, and even construction materials.
- **Waste-derived materials**: Some researchers are investigating ways to turn agricultural and industrial waste into new materials. For example, chitosan, a biopolymer derived from shrimp shells and other crustaceans, has shown potential for creating biodegradable films and coatings. Similarly, lignin, a byproduct of the paper and biofuel industries, can be used to create bioplastics.

The choice of raw material will depend on factors such as availability, processing requirements, and desired properties of the final product. By using renewable resources, inventors can reduce the environmental impact of material production and create alternatives to plastic that are part of a sustainable, circular economy.

4. Designing the Material's Molecular Structure

Once raw materials are selected, the next step is to design the molecular structure of the new material. This involves determining how the building blocks (such as monomers) will link together to form polymers with specific properties. The structure of the material will influence its strength, flexibility, biodegradability, and resistance to heat and moisture.

- **Polymerization**: Polymerization is the process of joining monomers together to create long chains, known as polymers. In the case of bioplastics, this process may involve combining plant-based or algae-based monomers into chains that mimic the properties of traditional plastics. The length and branching of these polymer chains will affect the material's strength, flexibility, and other properties.
- **Cross-linking**: Cross-linking refers to the process of creating connections between polymer chains, which can enhance the material's durability and resistance to breaking or deforming. However, excessive cross-linking can make a material more rigid and less biodegradable, so it is essential to strike a balance that allows for durability while still enabling the material to break down naturally in the environment.
- **Blending**: In some cases, blending different polymers together can create a composite material with enhanced properties. For example, blending PLA with other biopolymers can improve its flexibility, strength, and heat resistance, making it suitable for applications where pure PLA might fall short. Blending may also allow inventors to combine the advantages of multiple renewable materials, creating a more versatile plastic alternative.

The molecular design of the material will also need to consider how the material will degrade in the environment. Ideally, the material should break down into harmless organic compounds that can be absorbed by soil or water without leaving behind microplastics or toxic residues.

5. Testing and Refining Material Properties

Once a new material has been synthesized, it is essential to test its properties to ensure it meets the desired performance criteria. Testing should include assessments of:

- **Mechanical properties**: How strong and flexible is the material? Can it withstand stress and strain without breaking? Is it suitable for packaging, containers, or construction?
- **Thermal properties**: How does the material perform under different temperature conditions? Will it melt or degrade at high temperatures? Can it handle freezing or extreme heat without losing its structural integrity?
- **Biodegradability**: How long does the material take to break down under natural environmental conditions? Will it degrade into harmless organic matter, or will it leave behind harmful residues? Testing should simulate different environmental conditions, such as exposure to soil, water, and sunlight.
- **Toxicity**: Does the material leach harmful chemicals during its production, use, or decomposition? Biocompatibility is essential for materials that will come into contact with food, water, or the human body.

Testing is an iterative process, meaning the material may need to be refined and re-engineered multiple times to achieve the desired balance of strength, durability, and environmental friendliness. Additionally, testing in real-world conditions (such as landfill or marine environments) is crucial to understanding how the material will perform outside the laboratory.

6. Scaling Production and Commercialization

Once a viable material has been developed and tested, the next challenge is scaling up production. Small-scale laboratory production must be translated into large-scale manufacturing processes that can produce the material efficiently and cost-effectively.

- **Sourcing raw materials**: Sustainable sourcing of raw materials is critical to ensuring the environmental benefits of the new material are maintained at scale. This may involve cultivating renewable feedstocks such as algae or finding ways to use waste materials from other industries.
- **Manufacturing processes**: Scaling up production may require the development of new manufacturing techniques or the adaptation of existing processes. For example, if the new material is based on algae, processes for harvesting, drying, and processing algae into polymer precursors will need to be optimized. In some cases, manufacturers may need to invest in new equipment or facilities to accommodate the production of bioplastics or other sustainable materials.
- **Economic viability**: Ensuring economic viability is one of the most challenging aspects of creating a new material to replace plastic. While the environmental benefits are clear, the material must also be cost-competitive with conventional plastics to achieve widespread adoption. This involves considering several factors:

- **Cost of raw materials**: Renewable or biodegradable materials may be more expensive than petrochemical-based plastics, especially if they require extensive cultivation, harvesting, or processing. Innovations in material science can help reduce these costs, such as finding more efficient ways to grow and extract polymers from algae or plants.

- **Production efficiency**: The manufacturing process must be optimized for efficiency to reduce energy consumption, waste, and costs. This could involve improving polymerization techniques, reducing the need for energy-intensive processing, or designing more efficient molds and production lines for shaping the material.

- **End-of-life management**: One of the main advantages of creating a new material to replace plastic is its ability to biodegrade or be recycled. However, infrastructure for managing these new materials must be developed alongside the material itself. For example, compostable materials may require industrial composting facilities to break down properly, while recyclable alternatives may need new sorting and recycling systems. Ensuring that the material can be easily integrated into existing waste management systems, or incentivizing the development of new systems, will be critical to its success.

- **Market demand and consumer behavior**: Even if a material is economically viable and environmentally friendly, it must appeal to consumers. Public awareness of plastic pollution has been rising, and many consumers are willing to pay a premium for sustainable products. However, widespread adoption will likely require education about the benefits of the new material and clear labeling to differentiate it from conventional plastics. Governments may also play a role in stimulating demand through policies that encourage the use of biodegradable materials or ban single-use plastics.

Commercialization also involves navigating intellectual property, patents, and regulatory approvals. Inventors and companies must secure patents to protect their innovations and navigate regulatory frameworks that govern the safety and environmental impact of new materials. Collaborating with governments, NGOs, and industry partners can accelerate the adoption of new materials by ensuring compliance with environmental standards and fostering public support.

7. Case Studies of Emerging Plastic Alternatives

Several promising alternatives to plastic have already been developed, showcasing the potential for new materials to reduce environmental pollution:

- **Polylactic Acid (PLA)**: As one of the most widely used bioplastics, PLA is derived from fermented plant starch, usually from corn or sugarcane. PLA is biodegradable under industrial composting conditions, making it an attractive alternative for packaging, disposable tableware, and other single-use items. However, PLA is not suitable for all applications due to its lower heat resistance and slower degradation in natural environments. Further innovations in PLA blends and formulations are underway to enhance its properties and biodegradability.

- **Mycelium-based materials**: Mycelium, the root structure of fungi, can be used to create lightweight, durable materials with applications in packaging, insulation, and even fashion. Mycelium grows rapidly and is fully biodegradable, making it a sustainable alternative to plastic foam and other synthetic materials. Companies like Ecovative are already producing mycelium-based packaging, which has caught the attention of major brands looking to reduce their environmental footprint.

- **Seaweed-based bioplastics**: Seaweed is an abundant and fast-growing marine resource that can be harvested with minimal environmental impact. Researchers have developed bioplastics from seaweed polymers, which can be used for packaging, films, and other applications. These materials are biodegradable, and because they are sourced from marine environments, they offer a low-carbon alternative to land-based crops like corn or sugarcane. Seaweed-based packaging is already being used in food and beverage industries, demonstrating the material's potential for reducing plastic waste.

- **Chitosan**: Derived from the shells of shrimp and other crustaceans, chitosan is a natural polymer with antimicrobial properties. It can be used to create biodegradable films, coatings, and packaging materials. Since chitosan is derived from a waste product, it represents a sustainable option for plastic alternatives. However, the availability of chitosan is limited by the supply of crustacean shells, making it more suitable for niche applications rather than widespread use.

- **PHA (Polyhydroxyalkanoates)**: PHAs are biopolymers produced by microorganisms during the fermentation of sugars and fats. These materials are biodegradable and can be used in a variety of applications, from packaging to medical implants. PHA is more versatile than PLA, with higher heat resistance and a faster degradation rate in natural environments. However, its production costs are currently higher than conventional plastics, limiting its adoption to specialized markets. As research and production methods improve, PHA could become a more economically viable alternative to plastic.

These case studies illustrate the diversity of approaches being explored to replace plastic with sustainable, biodegradable materials. Each material has its own strengths and limitations, but collectively, they represent the potential for innovation in material science to tackle the global plastic pollution crisis.

8. The Future of Materials Science and Environmental Innovation

The development of new materials to replace plastic is not just about solving a current problem; it is about reimagining how materials are designed, produced, and disposed of in a more sustainable world. Future innovations in materials science will likely focus on several key areas:

- **Closed-loop systems**: Moving toward a circular economy, where materials are designed for reuse, recycling, and regeneration, will be critical to reducing environmental pollution. Future materials should be fully recyclable, compostable, or biodegradable, allowing them to be reintroduced into the environment without causing harm. Researchers are exploring ways to create materials that can be broken down and reassembled at the molecular level, enabling infinite reuse.

- **Biomimicry**: Nature offers countless examples of materials that are strong, flexible, and biodegradable. Biomimicry involves studying natural systems and replicating their properties in human-made materials. For example, spider silk is known for its strength and flexibility, and scientists are working to replicate its properties for use in textiles and medical devices. Biomimetic materials could offer an environmentally friendly alternative to synthetic plastics while enhancing performance.

- **Green chemistry**: Innovations in chemistry are enabling the creation of materials with minimal environmental impact. Green chemistry focuses on using non-toxic, renewable ingredients and processes to create materials that are safe for both people and the planet. This includes finding alternatives to toxic additives used in plastics, such as phthalates and BPA, and reducing the use of hazardous chemicals in material production.

- **Nanotechnology**: Advances in nanotechnology could allow for the development of materials with enhanced properties, such as increased strength, flexibility, or biodegradability. Nanomaterials could also be used to create coatings that repel water, dirt, or microbes, reducing the need for chemical treatments and enhancing the durability of products.

- Nanotechnology may also play a role in creating materials that can capture carbon or pollutants from the environment, helping to mitigate climate change and pollution.

As these fields evolve, the potential to create new materials that replace plastic will continue to grow. Collaboration between scientists, engineers, policymakers, and industries will be essential to ensuring that these innovations are adopted on a large scale and integrated into global supply chains.

OUTRO

The invention of a new material to replace plastic is not only an environmental necessity but also a complex scientific challenge that requires a multidisciplinary approach. By selecting sustainable raw materials, designing molecular structures for biodegradability and durability, testing and refining material properties, and scaling up production, innovators can develop materials that meet the functional demands of plastic while reducing pollution.

The success of these efforts will depend on factors such as cost-effectiveness, consumer acceptance, and the development of infrastructure for recycling or composting. However, the case studies of emerging alternatives show that progress is being made, and the potential for replacing plastic with environmentally friendly materials is within reach.

As materials science advances and new innovations emerge, the goal of reducing environmental pollution through sustainable alternatives to plastic is becoming more realistic. By continuing to explore new ideas, technologies, and collaborations, we can move closer to a world where plastic pollution is a problem of the past, and the materials we use are designed to coexist harmoniously with the natural environment.

ABOUT THE CREATOR

Walter the Educator is one of the pseudonyms for Walter Anderson. Formally educated in Chemistry, Business, and Education, he is an educator, an author, a diverse entrepreneur, and he is the son of a disabled war veteran. "Walter the Educator" shares his time between educating and creating. He holds interests and owns several creative projects that entertain, enlighten, enhance, and educate, hoping to inspire and motivate you. Follow, find new works, and stay up to date with Walter the Educator™

at WaltertheEducator.com

www.ingramcontent.com/pod-product-compliance
Lightning Source LLC
LaVergne TN
LVHW010414070526
838199LV00064B/5300